ONCE UPON A CHRISTMAS

By Roberta Simpson

ONCE UPON A CHRISTMAS

Published by Carpenter's Son Publishing, Franklin, Tennessee

Published in association with Larry Carpenter of Christian Book Services, LLC
www.christianbookservices.com

Printed in the United States of America by Worzalla.

ISBN-13: 978-0-615-32573-6

It has been a very exciting journey writing Once Upon a Christmas. The Christmas Story has been read and told countless times over a span of two thousand years, but it never gets boring. I believe that the Lord has inspired me in a special way to write this book, for which I am very grateful. After all, it is His story!

I hope that children everywhere will embrace this Christmas book and once again be thrilled reading the Greatest Story Ever Told, so I dedicate this book not only to my nine wonderful grandchildren, but to children everywhere. Our world is a much more exciting and better place because of our children. My prayer is that many will be blessed and filled with new hope and peace when they read this story.

May the Lord Bless and Keep You Always!

-Roberta Simpson, "Nana"

TABLE OF CONTENTS

ONCE UPON A CHRISTMAS

By Roberta Simpson

he Christmas story is a wonderful tale told all over the world to millions of children and grownups every year. I love it because it shows us how much God loves us, by sending His only son to Earth as a baby, where He grew up to show us the way to God. Or, as it says in that wonderful scripture, John 3:16, "For God so loved the world that He gave His only begotten Son that whosoever believes in Him shall not perish but have eternal life!"

So sit back and read the Christmas story as I imagine those who saw it happen might have told it.

EXCITEMENT
IN HEAVEN

id you hear what's going on? Something's up!" said Rafael, a young angel-in-training, whispering excitedly to his friend. "Something is going to happen that has never happened before!" "I agree," the angel beside him nodded. "I have never seen or heard so much excitement."

Those angels were just two of the hundreds moving up and down a lovely white staircase,

chatting excitedly, while flashes of the most beautiful colors streaked the air around them. The white of the angels' wings contrasted with the blue, green, red and purple of their outfits. Some wore colors that we could never describe because they only exist in the light of heaven.

At the top of the staircase, which seemed almost endless, white clouds billowed out like smoke. The angels came in every size and color. Some were massive warrior-angels over ten feet tall!

Above the chatter, a sound rose. It was the singing of angels praising their King. As they sang of their love for God, their voices sounded

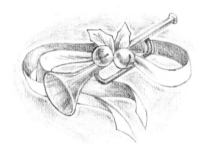

like a choir of bells and trumpets. The singing did not seem to bother the other angels who were studying scrolls and having lengthy discussions with one another. More than anything, it was clear that these majestic beings were in love with God, and they were filled with His purpose. Nothing was too hard or bothersome for them to do for Him.

A senior angel stood upon a high platform and said with authority, "Quiet, please. I wish to make an announcement." All noise stopped except for the soft rustle of wings as the angels waited to hear the news.

The two young angels pushed their way to the front of the crowd. They just had to learn what all the fuss was about.

"Something is going to happen tonight that will forever change the world. Our Lord and our God has a plan to heal and deliver the human race from sin, and we all remember when sin entered the world in the Garden of Eden! Our Lord is sending someone to take the blame for all of the bad things all the people have done. The one He is sending is His only Son, and tonight He will go to the earth as a baby and the world will never be the same! I need you to stand by and be ready, for a multitude of you will be chosen to go to earth and make a joyful noise, in praise to our God!"

There was silence only for a second, and then all of the angels began to speak at once. What wonderful and amazing news! Who would be chosen for the choir to announce the birth of the Savior?

The young angel in training could not contain himself, and shouted out loudly, "Oh, may I go? I want to go!" As soon as the words came out of his mouth he realized his mistake. The senior angel glared at him, but just before he hung his head, the young angel thought that just maybe he had seen a twinkle in the older angel's eye.

The senior angel discussed more details, and

the more he spoke, the more excitement

seemed to spread through Heaven. The more

enthusiastic the angels became, more amazing

music and glorious singing was heard, and

colorful lightning flashed until heaven was filled with the blinding beauty of the celebration.

So kids, can YOU imagine the excitement? Angels are a big part of God's Kingdom and you can read about them all through the Bible. They always obey God, and do His bidding. They are often messengers, and that night they had the best news of all to share. The angels were created as ministering spirits to attend to those who are heirs of salvation. They are there to do God's will!

THE INN

I n ancient times, around every fourteen years, the government would take a census. A census is when the government counts all the people of a country, and for this census everyone had to return to their hometown to be registered. That is why Joseph had to take Mary from Nazereth to Bethlehem. We know that Joseph and Mary could not find a place to stay, however, in the Bible we

see that an innkeeper let Joseph and Mary stay in his barn. I wonder what he and his family thought when they found out that the baby born on their property was Jesus, the promised Messiah? Maybe the innkeeper wished he'd given up his own room.

Netanya awoke bright and early. The sun was streaming through the window in the bedroom she shared with her four-year-old brother. It was

a tiny room in the attic, but very cozy and had a nice tree outside. With the sun shining through the trees into her room and the sweet little birds singing their "good morning" song for her, she felt happy and at peace.

Her family was not too well off. They ran a little inn, but very few people came to stay. That had all changed when the emperor declared a census, meaning people would soon be pouring into the tiny town of Bethlehem to be counted and registered. Netanya's father worried that they might not have enough rooms to house all the guests who would come to their inn for shelter.

Netanya stretched, thanked Adonai for a new day, and jumped out of bed. Because she was ten years old, she was expected to help her Mom and Dad with all of the preparations. She slipped her dress over her head and then she tugged a comb through her thick, curly dark hair. She kissed her little brother on top of the head and left him still sleeping while she ran down the stairs.

"I am glad to see that you are up," Netanya's mother said. "I need you to start preparing vegetables right away. We are expecting lots of people later, and they will all be hungry and want food." Netanya started in right away helping her mother. She sighed a little when she thought of the cleaning they would give each of the rooms. There was always such a

lot to do to prepare for guests.

Just then, her Daddy came into the kitchen.
"Well, I have fed all the animals and new hay
has been laid in the barn." He sat down in his
comfortable chair and said, "I am so thankful

for the census at times like this! We sure need the money, since the government takes advantage of us. Bethlehem is going to be a very busy little town in the days to come." Just then, Netanya's little brother came down the stairs, rubbing his sleepy eyes, and then she helped her mother by getting him his breakfast.

The day went fast, with friends and family bustling around and getting things ready. There were some arguments and tempers flared a couple of times, but all in all it was a good day. Netanya could hardly believe that there would be enough people to eat all of the food they'd made. By early afternoon everything was ready at last.

Soon enough, the first guests started to arrive.
There were old people and young people,
people with squealing children and elderly
people bent over with age. Some were rich but
most were poor, just ordinary people from every
walk of life.

By supper time, the inn was full. In fact, it was
so full that it looked like the little bedroom that
Netanya shared with her brother would be
used to house a couple with two small children.
That made Netanya a little glum, to think she
and her brother would have to spend the
night sleeping in blankets on the floor of their
parents' room.

The innkeeper and his family were just beginning to relax when they heard a knock on their locked door. Netanya's mother looked at the door in surprise. It was getting late and most of the guests had finished their supper by this time and were going to bed, exhausted from their travels.

Netanya was very sleepy, but the sound of the knock completely awakened her. Her father opened the door a little to see who could be there at this late hour, and Netanya peeped around her Daddy for a closer look.

A husband and wife were at the door. The wife was seated on a small, dusty-looking donkey

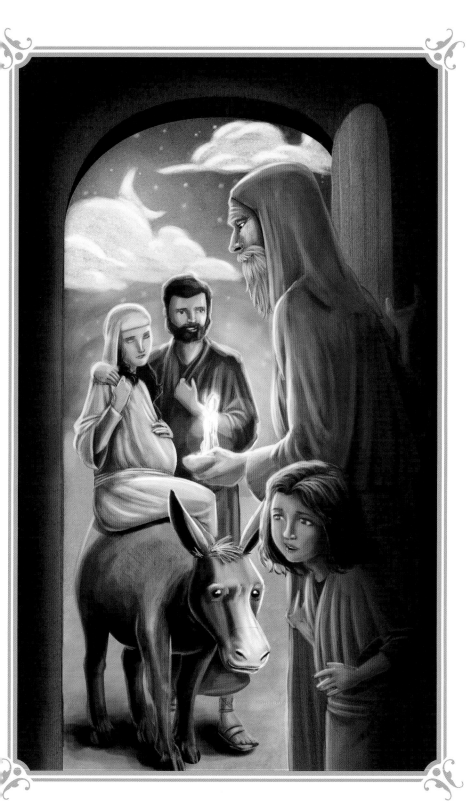

with a hand on her belly. She looked like she must be near to having her baby and she also looked very tired and uncomfortable. Netanya suddenly felt sad that her Daddy had already rented out her room. "Now we'll have to turn these poor people away. Oh I wish they could have stayed with us," she thought.

Her Dad spoke with the husband, whose name was Joseph. "I'm sorry, but we are full. We do not even have a corner in the house where you could stay." "But there are no inns around for miles," Joseph replied, his exhausted voice showing how tired he was. "My wife is about to have a baby and is most uncomfortable. Have you nowhere for us to stay?"

26

Netanya's father thoughtfully tugged at the beard on his chin. He hesitantly replied, "Well, we do have a barn. I put fresh hay down this morning and it is warm." "That will do just fine!" Joseph said quickly, before the innkeeper could change his mind.

It was Netanya's job to show them the way to the barn. She learned that the lady's name was Mary, and Netanya was able to find some warm milk and some bread for Mary and her husband. "I will see you in the morning," Netanya said to Joseph and Mary. "Goodnight," said Mary and Joseph as they smiled back at her.

Netanya ran back to the inn and went to bed, thinking about the wonderful couple in the barn. "I wonder when she will have the baby…" thought Netanya, but before she could finish the thought, she fell asleep. She was so exhausted that she slept soundly, even when the light of a bright new star came shining in through her window.

THE TRESPASSING DONKEY

an you imagine that God's only son, Jesus the Messiah, would be born in a barn, with lots of animals? Jesus – Prince, Messiah, King! What a lowly birth, born in the sight of animals. How amazing is that? Little did they know that there was a very exciting event about to happen that night – an event that lowly animals would witness before even any human. I wonder what the animals would

have thought... We can get an idea from this part of the story.

Inside the small barn behind the inn, a few hours before Joseph and Mary arrived, the animals in the barn were having an argument. The cow had started complaining. She complained about the food, she complained about the barn, and she even complained about all the animals around her, as if she were the queen and they were all her subjects. Of course, the other animals got tired of her attitude.

"Will you just keep quiet?" said the large red rooster with beautiful green tail feathers. The

horse chimed in,
swishing his long
black tail back
and forth, "You are
so ungrateful! You're

warm and well fed, your owner lets you rest

and laze around, and he only comes to you for

milk twice a day! Most of your kind live in fear

for their lives!" he snorted loudly, and turned

his back on her. "She could have been our

owner's dinner!" All the animals then turned on

the cow and quarreled with her, each in their

own loud voice, until the barn sounded like a

zoo at feeding time. They should have all been

ashamed of themselves!

Only the sheep tried to defend her. "Oh, you poor dear. You must be having a bad day. Can I be of any help?" said the sheep, as she inched her white, wooly body closer to where the cow was standing. The cow stuck her head into the air without answering, and nearly swiped the poor sheep with her tail.

Just then, they heard a disturbance. Someone was approaching the barn. Thinking it could have been the innkeeper, who looked after them so well, they all perked up and pretended everything was fine.

The hen flew to the top of the barn's door and peered out. "There is a donkey coming!" she cried. "Oh, and there are two humans with him, and the lady human has a very large tummy! She must be about to have a baby! Silly humans! Laying eggs is much easier, I'm sure."

On top of a pile of hay, the cat groomed himself and haughtily said, "We do not need any more animals in here. We certainly don't need a donkey. If he comes in here, he's trespassing!" Most of the other animals nodded in agreement. After all, the barn was not that big and another large animal would take up quite a lot of room.

The strangers were led in by Netanya, who then disappeared back to the inn. The man spread

his cloak on the clean hay and helped his wife

lie down, then he made sure the donkey was

fed and watered. At last, after eating some

bread and milk, the man and woman put out

the small oil lamp that lit up the barn before

closing their eyes.

"Psst. What are you doing here?" the hen clucked softly to the donkey. The donkey replied, "Oh, am I tired! You've got a nice barn. I'm so glad to finally rest my hooves and my poor back. I've been walking almost non-stop for hours and hours." He looked around again, shook his mane and said, "As I said before, you sure have got a nice barn, but my wonderful owners don't belong here."

"Where did you come from?" the animals asked, and they all leaned in to hear the newcomer's answer. The donkey lay down and hung his head. "We came from Nazareth. It was a long and dangerous journey. Sometimes robbers attack travelers on that road. I'm just glad we got here safely." He yawned widely and said, "Excuse me, can we talk later? Right now I just want to rest."

"Of course. Sleep well," whispered the sheep. There was something special about this donkey, and all the animals had warmed up to him.

The animals settled down and the barn grew quiet. There was not a sound except for the breathing of the animals, the chirping of crickets, and the whispering of the young couple on the straw.

In the middle of the night the animals were awakened by a strange noise that sounded something like the mewing of a kitten. When the animals looked, they saw an amazing sight: a tiny baby boy lay in his mother's arms. Never had the animals thought that people would spend the night in their barn, and they certainly never expected a baby to be born there. They all felt a strange joy at the sight of the infant. Something was different – special – about this child.

Mary and Joseph smiled and cooed to the baby, who they had named Jesus. Two kittens that had been sleeping near the cow's hooves eased closer to the baby, but Joseph put up a hand just in time to stop them from giving the baby a friendly lick, and eventually the little

family fell fast asleep. In the darkness the cow turned to the horse and whispered, "I'm sorry I was complaining so much. Will you forgive me?" The horse answered "Yes" in a soft, rumbling voice. "I was wrong for getting mad and saying mean things to you." He laid his head over the cow in a horsey version of a hug. The sheep smiled to herself as a comforting peace settled over the barn.

THE SHEPHERDS

ou see, children, Israel had been occupied by the Romans for many years and life was very hard for the Jewish people. They longed to be free. Free to worship as Jews, free to live as God's people, free to bring up their children as they should, and not have to live in fear of the Romans. So imagine what it must have been like for the shepherds who were watching their sheep on those dark hills outside of

Bethlehem so long ago. What a shock to witness the sky light up and the hills ring with the amazing sounds of multitudes of angels!

Hagai was so excited! He was only twelve years old, and he could not wait for the evening to start. It would be the first time that he would go with his Dad to mind the sheep. His friend Caleb was also there with his Dad. Hagai straightened his tunic and tried to look like a grownup. Caleb saw Hagai and he tried to make himself look taller by standing on a small rock.

The sun sank behind the hills and darkness fell, giving way to a beautiful, clear night. They could see hundreds of stars in the sky shining so brilliantly that the boys almost felt that they could reach out and touch them. Each of the shepherds carried his supper in a small bundle and they ate and chatted near the flock. Hagai and Caleb sat together a little distance away from the older men, both boys alert to the danger all around them. How many times had their fathers told them stories about wolves or lions gobbling up a sheep? They didn't want to be too far away from their fathers in case something like that happened.

It was a beautiful, clear night where hundreds of stars could be seen in the sky. As they broke bread together and asked Yaweh to bless their meal, the elders started to talk about their

favorite subject: their Messiah. These Jewish

men loved to discuss scripture and they would

debate many topics, but their most frequent

discussion of all was about the Messiah. When

would He come? How much longer would they

have to wait? Would He come and fight their

enemies, the Romans? Sometimes they argued, but they never stayed angry at each other for long.

With their stomachs full and the sheep happily feeding nearby, Josia lay down on the grassy hill, with the other shepherds. He put his hands behind his head, looking up at the most magnificent night.

"What a night this is!" he said. "I can't believe how clear the sky is. I feel sorry for all those townspeople under their roofs."

"It certainly is beautiful!" said Zack. "And it is so quiet and peaceful. At times like these, I can almost forget all about our troubles."

"Well I can't!" said Joshua. "Only today my son and I had to run from the Romans. We had done nothing! They called us 'filthy Jews' and began chasing us. I want the Messiah to come now and bring His sword, to rid us of all the Romans!" Hagai and Caleb listened, shuddering as they remembered that not too long ago, they too had been chased by the Romans.

"You have it all wrong, Joshua," said Samuel. "Some of us have been studying the scriptures concerning the Messiah. Aaron, tell us what you read this morning."

Excitedly, Aaron replied, "I read from Isiah today. The scripture said that when the Messiah comes, He will be full of the spirit of the Sovereign Lord. He is going to preach the Good News to the poor and the broken-hearted!"

"Yes!" said Josia. "And He is going to set the captives free, and comfort all who mourn."

Samuel added, "Remember, the prophecies say that He will heal the sick, raise the dead, and open the eyes of the blind and the ears of the deaf!"

"Wow!" said Zach. "How wonderful is that?"

Joshua did not look too happy. He did not disagree with his friends, but he muttered under his breath, "I still want Him to kill off the Romans!"

Hosea added, "Do you know the scriptures say that the Messiah would be born in Bethlehem?" That led into a lot of lively discussion, but eventually the shepherds started to feel a little tired and fell silent. The older shepherds pretended not to notice the gentle snores. Hagai and Caleb sat side by side, with their arms around their knees and their heads resting on their arms. The boys had not missed a

word, and they felt excited from all the talk.
It was such a special night, full of expectancy
and miracles.

Meanwhile, in Heaven the activity had
increased. Angels were being summoned from
all over and were getting ready to descend to
earth, to be a part of the most wonderful event
that had ever happened.

Standing next to two of his friends, Rafael,
the young Angel in training, was holding his
breath. "Oh, please, oh, please!" he muttered
under his breath. "I want to go!" Suddenly,
the chief angel turned to him and said, "You
three are going!" All three of the young angels

shouted in delight, and as they joined the crowd preparing to depart they received some stern looks from some of the older angels. They waited for the signal and looked down through the floor of heaven to the waiting earth below. Then, when they heard the blast of a trumpet, all of the angels swooped down like a huge flock of shining eagles.

The shepherds leapt to their feet as a blinding light pierced the darkness, and at its center there appeared an angel of the Lord. The shepherds were terrified! They all fell to their knees before the dazzling sight and knelt, speechless and shaking in the grass, as the angel began to speak.

"Do not be afraid!" the angel said to them, "Because I am here announcing to you Good News that will bring great joy to all the people. This very day, in the town of David, there was born for you a deliverer who is the Messiah, the Lord. Here is how you will know Him: you will find a baby wrapped in cloth, lying in a feeding trough."

Suddenly, the whole sky lit up and all the shepherds could see was a vast army of angels. They were all praising God and saying, "In the highest Heaven, glory to God! And on earth, peace among people of good will!"

As suddenly as the angels had appeared,

they flew back up to Heaven, and for a few moments the shepherds lay motionless in shock. Shortly, Joshua spoke and said, "Let's go over to Bethlehem and see this wondrous thing that that Yaweh has told us has happened."

"Pick up your pack quickly!" whispered Caleb to Hagai. "We don't want to be left behind to tend the sheep while the others go to see the Messiah!"

"Don't worry, son," laughed Andrew. "No one will be left behind tonight. How could we deny you boys the chance of a lifetime?" So they all went, singing every psalm of praise to God they could think of, all the way to Bethlehem.

I just cannot imagine how they felt. Shepherds were the most despised of all peoples at that time, and yet God had ordained His angels to appear and speak to them. Their lives would never again be the same.

THE FIRST VISITORS

t was the early hours of the morning, and all was quiet in the barn. The newborn baby – Yeshua – Jesus started to stir. His eyes opened wide, and His little hands started to wave around. Mary, who was sleeping lightly, woke up. She picked up her precious baby and held Him close in her arms. She smiled at Him and softly said, "How adorable You are!" She was sure He smiled back, but could such young infants actually smile?

She began to sing to Him. One by one all of the animals awoke to hear Mary singing with her beautiful voice to her little boy. The two little kittens woke up and tried to come closer to the baby. He smelled so good, and they loved the faint scent of milk on Him. Mary smiled at them, but turned the baby slightly away so they couldn't reach Him.

Mary nuzzled the baby's cheek and said, "I remember when the angel Gabriel appeared to me and announced that God had chosen me to be the mother of His only Son, and now here You are. Did you know that the same angel appeared to your Daddy? He told him not to worry and the angel told him your name, little Jesus." She whispered a prayer, "Yaweh, I am so grateful for all You have done. Please help us raise this special child."

Just then, Joseph awoke. He stretched and saw that Mary was awake and holding Jesus. He jumped to his feet with a big smile on his face and said, "Oh, I had a wonderful rest! Now let me hold the baby and then I'll see about getting us something to eat and drink." He took Jesus from Mary, and buried his face in the baby's tummy. The baby squirmed and giggled His enjoyment.

Joseph stopped and turned his head to listen to the sound of several male voices. He put the

baby down into his little feedbox manger and

as he listened the sound of voices came closer.

Then the door of the barn opened and a group

of men and a pair of young boys walked in.

Mary studied them with concern, but their

faces reassured her that they were friendly. She knew at once they were shepherds, but she had no idea what they were doing in the barn.

The shepherds didn't even notice the new parents; they only had eyes for the baby lying in the manger. "It's just like the angel said," whispered Hagai. The other shepherds nodded. Josia had tears running down into his beard. The shepherds all fell to their knees before the baby. "The Messiah!" they said.

Mary and Joseph looked at each other in wonder, and then Joseph said, "Who has told you this?" Samuel spoke first, "An angel told us last night that the Messiah had been born in Bethlehem. He said we would find Him wrapped up and lying in a manger."

"Then the sky was filled with angels praising God," Caleb interrupted eagerly. "They turned the night as bright as day, and I thought I was going to die from fright. Then the angels disappeared as quickly as they had come."

Andrew continued, "We walked as fast as we could to get here, and now we see that the angel's words are true. There He is, just as the angel said. The Messiah has come at last and we have lived to see all the hopes of our people fulfilled!"

The shepherds' words filled Mary and Joseph with amazement. Joseph said wistfully, "I can't imagine what it would have been like to see so many angels. I have only seen one angel in a dream, and I was overwhelmed with fear and wonder."

Joseph and Mary were sharing their story with the shepherds when Mary looked up to see Netanya and her friend coming through the door with food. Netanya had seen the shepherds approaching. She had brought bread, cheese, nuts and fruit. Water and fresh milk from the cow completed the feast.

Netanya was so delighted to see the newborn baby that she nearly dropped her jug of milk. "Oh!" she cried. She looked at Mary with pleading eyes and said, "He is so sweet. May I hold Him?" "Of course," Mary answered. "Why don't you hold Him while we eat?"

Netanya tenderly took the baby, moved over to a stack of hay, and sat down with the little King. Her friend sat beside her and they gently played with Him. The others broke bread together and gave thanks to Yaweh for all of their blessings – especially for the blessing of Jesus, the promised Messiah.

After a while the girls remembered their chores and Netanya turned to Hagai, who was standing nearby watching the baby. "Do you want to hold Him?" she asked. Hagai quickly put his hands behind his back, saying "No thank you. I'll just watch." Netanya gave a merry laugh and the girls scampered back to the inn. Of course before they started their chores, they had to make sure that everyone at the inn knew about the new baby born in the barn!

"Thank you for letting us see the child," said Andrew as the shepherds prepared to go. "We will leave you now. We want to tell this wonderful news to our friends and family. We are witnesses to God's blessing."

As soon as the shepherds left the barn, they immediately started to tell everyone they saw about the special baby – the Messiah, the Deliverer who would bring salvation to His people! Everyone who heard them was amazed. Many of the villagers believed the wonderful news and praised God.

Later the Shepherds returned to their sheep in the fields, praising God for all the things they had heard and seen, which were just as the angel had told them. Hagai and Caleb certainly had quite a story to tell about their first night as real shepherds!

The greatest event in history had just happened! The Messiah had been born! For ages, Jewish people had waited for this, and when it finally occurred, the announcement came to humble shepherds. The good and wonderful news about Jesus is that He comes to all, including the humble and the ordinary. He comes to anyone with a heart open enough to accept Him. Whoever you are, whatever you do, you can have Jesus in your life. Don't think you have to be extra good or smart or pretty or strong – Jesus accepts you as you are!

THE WISE MEN

e just heard how God announced Jesus's birth to the common people, the shepherds. Now I want to tell you how God announced that wonderful news to the powerful people of the time. You may have heard of the Wise Men who came to see baby Jesus. Not much is known about these Magi – Wise Men — but some believe they were Kings from the East, each representing a different

nation. Tradition says they were men of high position from Parthia, near ancient Babylon, which today is Iraq. They may have been Jewish, or if not, men who somehow knew the prophecies of the scriptures. Imagine how excited they were to see a brand new star, brighter than all the rest, suddenly begin shining in the sky! They recognized that star as a sign that a new king had been born – a great king – and they eagerly set out on a journey to find Him.

The census was over and most people had gone back to their towns and villages, but Joseph and his little family decided to stay in Bethlehem. Netanya's parents helped Joseph

and Mary find a house, and Netanya helped
with the Baby when she had finished her
chores. Life settled into a happy routine and
Mary and Joseph were grateful for each day
together with their tiny son. But in a city far from
Jerusalem, things were beginning to happen
that would affect their small family.

In that faraway city there lived a great ruler
named Darius, who was rich and influential,
and he was a man of great kindness. Years
before he had heard about a small boy who
had been left alone, and the boy probably
would have starved if it weren't for Darius; the
boy's name was Shazar, and Darius took the
boy in to be one of his servants.

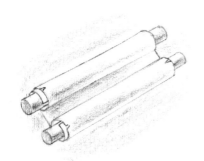

Darius was also a great scholar. Almost every night when Shazar brought him his dinner, he was bent over some scroll of the scriptures. Darius and his friends would often meet to study the stars and the scrolls and talk for hours about the Messiah who would soon be born in Israel.

One day when Shazar was fifteen, some of Darius's friends came to his palace very early in the morning and called for Shazar to get Darius at once. Before Shazar could even leave to get him, Darius came down to greet the visitors. He was just as excited as they were. Something wondrous had happened the night before, and they had spotted a magnificent star in the east that they had never seen before.

"Shazar!" he shouted loudly, with a big smile on his face. "Get ready. We are going to Jerusalem and we will leave this afternoon. Get the camels saddled and prepare as much food and water as you can. While studying the scriptures last night, my friends and I gathered together and saw the star we have sought for years. Hurry now, we have no time to lose."

Shazar moved quickly, passing orders on to other servants and making ready what he could, and the servants worked frantically to please their master because he was such a good man. Happily, all was ready at the appointed time.

Shazar had never been on such a long journey before. The caravan was on the road for so many days that he lost count. The journey was often hot, dusty and dangerous, and a few times robbers tried to stop them, but Shazar helped the other servants fight them off. These wise men were very wealthy, and they were bringing rich gifts, so any band of thieves would have been overjoyed at such plunder.

Just when it seemed to Shazar that they must have traveled to the end of the world, they

THE WISE MEN

reached Jerusalem at last. It was a beautiful

city, bustling with activity and filled with people.

The travelers approached the Jewish temple

and there Darius inquired of one of the priests,

"Where is the one who has been born King of the Jews? We saw his star in the east and have come to worship him!"

Shazar was astonished at the uproar that question caused. The travelers discovered that King Herod was the ruler of Israel at the time and everyone was very disturbed by the idea that another king had been born. No doubt Herod was afraid that the new king would take his place.

The priests must have sent a messenger to Herod, because not long after the caravan arrived, the king and some of his servants arrived from the palace and spoke to some of the priests that Darius had questioned. As the priests spoke, the king's face became very red. In fact, it became so red that Shazar thought Herod would burst!

Suddenly King Herod looked up and saw Darius and his companions. His eyes widened when he saw their rich robes and the camels standing behind them, loaded with expensive wares. The king seemed to forget his anger and when he walked toward them his smile was charming, but something about that smile did not seem genuine. Shazar did not trust him.

Herod spoke to Darius, saying, "I have asked my advisors and they say that the child is supposed to be born in Bethlehem. Go and find the child and then come back and tell me where he is. I also wish to worship Him." The wise men didn't know it, but the king was lying. Herod really wanted to have the child killed, so he could keep on being the King of the Jews.

After the king left, the wise men turned their caravan toward Bethlehem. It was easy finding the way because the same bright star led them. Eventually the trail stopped over a house in Bethlehem.

It seemed strange to Shazar that a great King would live in such a humble little house, but Darius and his friends were sure they had found the right place. They had traveled far and long

following the star because these wise men had

read the scriptures, and knew that this star

was the sign of the Messiah that the prophets

had written about, and there was great joy

among them.

"Now we can see Him for ourselves, and

worship Him!" Darius said to his friends as they

got down from their camels. All of them stood

behind Shazar eagerly as he went to the door

and knocked.

Netanya let them in. Her eyes were as big as

saucers as she stared at the richly dressed

men and servants standing at the door.

Remembering her manners, she introduced them to Mary. Mary led them to where the little boy sat on a small blue blanket. There was something about this little toddler that was different and wonderful, and young though He was, He smiled at them as if He knew them and His smile lit up His little face.

"Here He is! The true King! Praise be to the God of the Heavens!" exclaimed the wise men when they saw Jesus. Then the most astonishing thing happened: those rich, important men knelt on the floor of the little house and worshiped the Son of God. Even in their fancy robes, they humbled themselves before this small child. All of the servants knelt too. Shazar

didn't completely understand what was happening but he had a feeling that he was part of something important.

Still kneeling, the wise men called for the servants to bring them the gifts that they had brought. These great men then lay the gifts at Jesus' feet, and they gave him gold which represented royalty, frankincense, a gift usually given to a god, and myrrh which was usually given to one who was about to die. Although these were rich gifts fit for a king, they seemed strange to Shazar.

After the gifts were given, the caravan didn't spend much time in Bethlehem, and for the first time Shazar wished he could stay behind when his beloved master left. Shazar found that he loved the infant and wanted to stay around that special little child. They all did. However, Darius and his companions had responsibilities in their own land that could wait no longer.

As they prepared to leave, Darius called to his companions, "We must find a different route, one that does not include Jerusalem. Last night an angel spoke to me in a dream and warned me that Herod intends to harm the child. We must not tell him where he can find Jesus." "I too had such a dream," exclaimed one companion. "And I," said another. Several of the company told of similar dreams.

Shazar was relieved. He hadn't trusted Herod, but he hadn't dared tell anyone. Now little Jesus would surely be safe from the jealous king.

Shazar rode his donkey beside his master's camel as they slowly plodded out of Bethlehem. He thought of the journey and of the special baby King who lived in that tiny house. He knew he had been part of the event of a lifetime, and he knew he would never be the same again!

When the wise men didn't return, Herod decided to send his soldiers to find Jesus in Bethlehem, but God warned Joseph in a dream to leave right away with his family and go to Egypt because of Herod's evil plans for the holy infant. The family stayed in Egypt until Herod died, and it was safe to go return to Bethlehem.

So children, this is the way I think the Christmas story would have been told by the people who were there. Jesus was very special because He was God's only son. He grew up to be a man but He never did anything wrong. He healed the sick and told people about God. Then, because He loved you and me, He died to pay the penalty for all of the bad things we do. He loves you and He wants to forgive you for your sins so you can go to heaven and be with Him forever. There was no room at the inn for Jesus when He was about to be born, but the most important thing is: Is there room in your heart for Him?

ROBERTA SIMPSON
"Nana"

Born in London, England to a Princess* and a Jewish Big Band leader, Roberta Simpson has known a life filled with both privilege and persecution. Her family tree is filled with gifted musicians, artists, authors—and even a Russian boot maker! Roberta draws upon this rich heritage for her storytelling. Yet, the foundation for her original stories is her desire to teach children about the love of Jesus and the excitement of the Bible.

Roberta's love of storytelling began long ago when her young children preferred listening to her stories rather than those in books. She continued the tradition with her nine grandchildren and family friends who were always eager to hear stories from "Nana." After ignoring numerous requests through the years to have her stories published, Roberta believes the Lord called her to share her passion.

The growth of Roberta's faith in Jesus has been closely linked with children. Roberta's relationship with the Lord began during the saddest period in her life— while suffering the loss of a child. During this time, she started reading the Bible and through it developed an appreciation of God's creation, as well as an acceptance of her Jewish heritage. Roberta then totally committed her life to serving Jesus when her oldest daughter was hit by a car. She cried out to the Lord, "Take my whole life—do whatever you want to do in me!" The Lord has been using Roberta in amazing ways ever since—a TV host, playwright, songwriter, Bible teacher and now author!

Roberta's first book, Nana's Bible Stories, was published by Thomas Nelson in 2007. Nana's Bible Stories captures the warmth and wisdom of Scripture in a treasure of tales from the Bible. In it, Roberta weaves stories of courage, healing, hope, giving, salvation, and more while bringing the heart of God alive to young hearts. For more information, go to www.Nanasbiblestories.com.

Roberta resides in Barbados with her husband, Sir Kyffin Simpson, who was given the title of Commander of the British Empire by Queen Elizabeth in 2004 and then knighted in 2007.

*Sir James Brooke, an adventurer on the high seas, quelled a rebellion in Borneo. The Sultan gave Sarawak to him as a reward. Years later, his great-nephew, Sir Charles Vyner Brooke, and his wife, Lady Sylvia Brooke (Roberta's grandmother), assumed the reign as the Rajah and Ranee of Sarawak. Roberta's mother was known as Princess Pearl.

Roberta's grandmother was also a talented writer who was mentored by J.M. Barry. She was the inspiration for the character, "Wendy", in Barry's infamous PETER PAN.